Architectural Rendering in Tempera

Architectural Rendering in Tempera

....

RICHARD C. BAEHR

VAN NOSTRAND REINHOLD
I(T)P   A Division of International Thomson Publishing Inc.

New York • Albany • Bonn • Boston • Detroit • London • Madrid • Melburne
Mexico City • Paris • San Francisco • Singapore • Tokyo • Toronto

Acknowledgments

I wish to acknowledge the powerful influence of the Cooper Union on my career. The school of Art and Architecture being tuition free, accepts applications by competitive entry exam, resulting in a student body of exceptionally high caliber with no exceptions. One is surrounded by people of intelligence and wit, imagination and drive as well as a faculty of the highest quality. Unique among them was the late Richard G. Stein whose design philosophy and value system helped form the foundation of my professional development. Finally, I wish to thank my editor, Sherrel Farnsworth, for her professional skills and total tireless dedication in the development of this book.

Page ii: Da Nang Plaza, Shenzen, China. Angelo Frances Corva and Associates.
Page viii: 345 Hudson Street, New York City. Berg and Forster, Architects. This rendering is the winner of the Syd Mead Juror's Award, 1992, American Society of Architectural Perspectivists.
Page 20: 80 John Street, New York City. Buchman and Kahn, Architects. Rehabilitation: Zar Realty Management Corp.

I(T)P™ Van Nostrand Reinhold is an International Thomson Publishing company.
ITP logo is a trademark under license.

Printed in Hong Kong
For more information, contact:

Van Nostrand Reinhold
115 Fifth Avenue
New York, NY 10003

International Thomson Publishing GmbH
Königswinterer Str. 418
53227 Bonn
Germany

International Thomson Publishing Europe
Berkshire House,168-173
High Holborn
London WC1V 7AA
England

International Thomson Publishing Asia
221 Henderson Road. #05-10
Henderson Building
Singapore 0315

Thomas Nelson Australia
102 Dodds Street
South Melbourne 3205
Victoria, Australia

International Thomson Publishing Japan
Hirakawacho Kyowa Building, 3F
2-2-1 Hirakawacho
Chiyoda-ku, 102 Tokyo
Japan

Nelson Canada
1120 Birchmount Road
Scarborough, Ontario
Canada M1K 5G4

Internatioal Thomson Editores
Campos Eliseos 385, Piso 7
Col. Polanco
11560 Mexico D.F. Mexico

1 2 3 4 5 6 7 8 9 10 CP 01 00 99 98 97 96 95 94

Library of Congress Cataloging in Publication Data

Baehr, Richard C., 1930–
    Architectural rendering in tempera / by Richard C. Baehr.
        p. cm.
    Includes index.
    ISBN 0-442-01261-6
    1. Architectural rendering. 2. Tempera painting. I. Title.
NA2780.B34 1993
720′ .28′4—dc20   93-27897
                                                        CIP

*To Bob Schwartz, whose creativity
and innovations in the tempera
medium advanced architectural
rendering in color to a new
high standard of excellence*

Author's Note

Perhaps the main reason for writing a book of this kind is to record for present and future practitioners, one renderer's belief system in the art of illustrating architecture. The very process of writing a book draws out virtually all of the ideas one has ever had on the subject and makes them available now and into the future. The reader can make his or her judgements on the tempera medium versus the alternatives and use or discard any of the ideas discussed. The hope is that tempera will gain in popularity as a result of this effort.

Contents

1 . . . .

Tempera

■ Stan Getz once said: "I never played a note I didn't mean." It would be nice to be able to say the same about brush strokes, but with tempera, if you don't mean it, you can change it. This isn't the *main* advantage of tempera, just one that makes it a preferred medium for architectural rendering.

Tempera is the general term that includes all opaque water-based paints, for example, designer colors and poster colors. The name derives from egg tempera paints which were originally prepared with egg yolks as a medium instead of oil. Modern tempera uses substances such as gum arabic and water to achieve the results obtained by the egg yolk.

Gouache (pronounced *gwash*) is another name for tempera, although it refers more properly to the technique of applying transparent watercolors with opaque white. Any transparent watercolor paint can be used in a gouache technique.

Acrylic paint is the modern cousin of tempera. It has the same opaquing qualities, pigments, and consistency; you can work acrylic the same way as tempera with a bit more effort. It produces the same style of rendering. Because acrylic is plastic based, however, rendering with acrylic leaves little room for interruption. Brushes harden and palette colors, once dry, cannot be rejuvenated. The upside, of course, is that an acrylic rendering is less vulnerable to water damage. I have not switched to acrylics because it seems to me that tempera has most all the advantages of acrylics with none of the problems. Still, many of the rendering methods described here could be used just as easily for acrylics.

In general, tempera paints are watercolors that have extra ground to provide a greater degree of opacity. Poster colors, which are used primarily to cover broad, flat areas, need to be quite opaque and have the most ground. Designers colors have the least ground and the greatest purity. They mix with the greatest accuracy of any paints in this group.

Tempera paints can be purchased in tubes, jars, and cups at various prices. Designers colors produced by the top manufacturers of art supplies are the best quality, and the cost is comparatively high. These paints tend to dry out quickly, even in their containers, and must be used within a relatively short time after their purchase. Tubes should be checked at the store to be sure they aren't old. I find paint in jars much easier and less time-consuming to use.

As with all media, there is no substitute for experience in mastering the use of tempera. At first, it's difficult to get the right proportion of water and paint to run a sky, for example. Even after some time, the results you seek may still elude you. The beauty of tempera is that with experience, if you know what you've done doesn't meet your standards, you can paint it over. It's one of the few media in rendering today in which an entire building, if redesigned, can be repainted on the same board without redoing the entire rendering (see Figures 1–1 and 1–2).

Tempera, in my view, is simply the best medium for a literal, dramatic representation of architecture. It reproduces well in black and white and is especially favored by marketing oriented owners, developers, and advertising agencies.

Figure 1-1.
When the city of San Francisco rejected the original design (this page) as too tall, a second design (opposite page) was developed and substituted in the rendering.

Figure 1-2.
This revised design
for the city of San
Francisco office
building was painted
directly over the pre-
vious rendering.
Johnson and Burgee
Architects.

2 . . . .

Perspective Layout

■ It would be hard to exaggerate the importance of an excellent, perspective line drawing on which to base the tempera painting. Often one sees published renderings adequately executed in whatever medium, but based on a badly flawed perspective. Whether it's one of the classic mistakes—getting too close in an aerial view with the result that the foreground is "falling off the table" or a horizon that splits the building in two, or an angle not quite right—the rendering can't be successful if the *view* is wrong.

At the first meeting, the project designer usually indicates how the building should be seen. Before settling on the view other options should be explored. Sometimes a thumbnail sketch at the initial meeting is useful to confirm the understanding. Composition of the rendering can be discussed at this point—for example, trees, foreground elements, street activity. Now the creation of the mechanical perspective can begin.

As shown in Figure 2–1, a print of the appropriate plan is placed on the table at a distance and angle to the station point that will produce a perspective matching the thumbnail sketch. The client should receive a print of this block layout to OK so you can proceed with the rendering. On occasion I have faxed sketches to the architects and *their* clients at the same time so they can discuss them before I continue. A print of the finished perspective can be sent later as well. In actual practice, all of these steps are seldom necessary. The final step in the layout process is the transfer of the perspective to the illustration board for painting. This will be discussed later.

Construction of the Line Perspective

Most renderers still don't use the computer for perspective work. It is only used if the architectural firm already has the project data entered in its computer and can easily generate perspectives. Entering the data in the computer can be prohibitively time-consuming.

The projection method described in Figure 2–1 is familiar to *most* renderers. Here we'll discuss the use of the *centrolinead* for faraway vanishing points. The centrolinead or perspective T-square has a function similar to that of a standard T-square, except that with its adjustable arms it glides up and down against 5/8-inch push pins stuck into the table (see Figures 2–1 & 2–2).

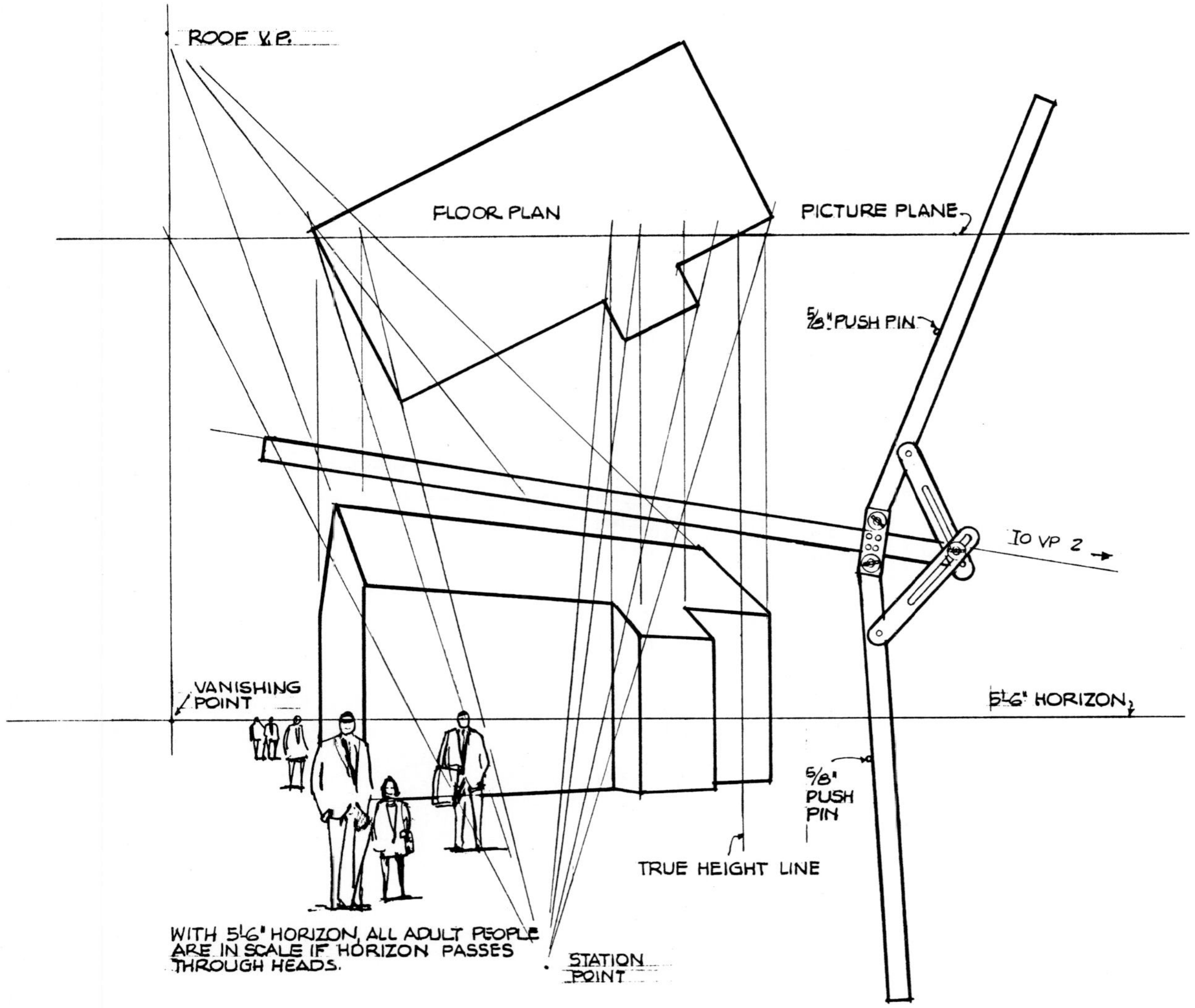

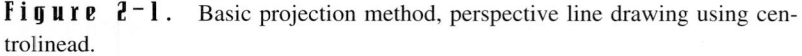

ROOF V.P.

FLOOR PLAN

PICTURE PLANE

⅝" PUSH PIN

TO VP 2 →

VANISHING POINT

5'6" HORIZON

⅝" PUSH PIN

TRUE HEIGHT LINE

WITH 5'6" HORIZON, ALL ADULT PEOPLE ARE IN SCALE IF HORIZON PASSES THROUGH HEADS.

STATION POINT

Figure 2-1.   Basic projection method, perspective line drawing using centrolinead.

In the layout process, the more distant vanishing point line is established using the nearby vanishing point (see the lower left side of the illustration above). We now have the horizon and one or two long vanishing point lines in the sky. The centrolinead arm is lined up on the horizon and push pins are stuck in the board inside the adjustable arms. (Holes can be made in the plastic board cover since they heal or almost disappear after the push pin is removed.) The centrolinead arm is then moved up to the long vanishing point lines. If the angle is way off, its arms can be adjusted. If it's close, the pins

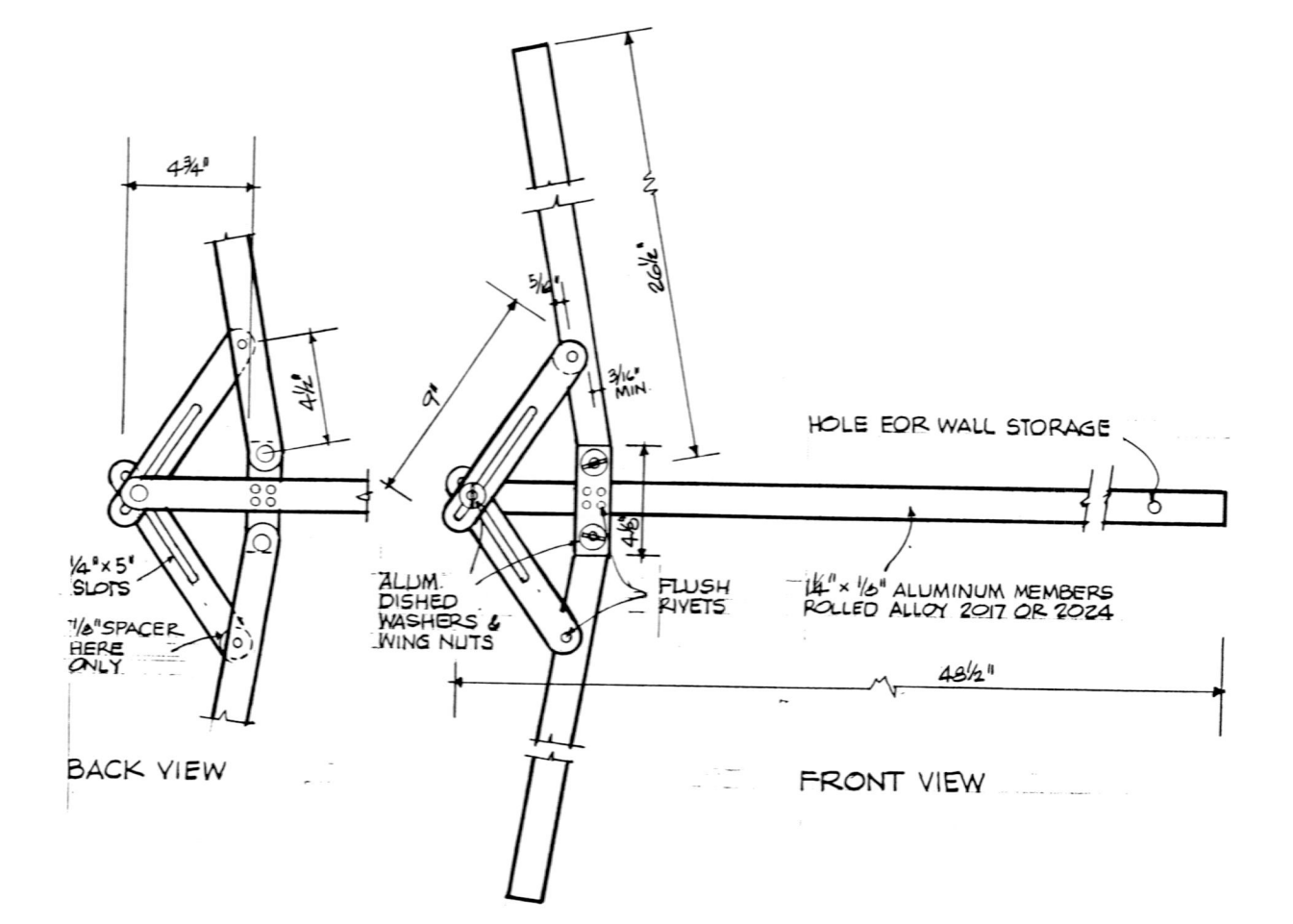

Figure 2-2. Descriptive drawing of a centrolinead.

are moved outward to flatten the angle and inward to sharpen it. You refine the angle until the long arm, if moved up or down, lines up with both the horizon and perspective lines. This creates a perspective T-square for drawing all the horizontal lines in relation to the more distant vanishing point, and of course the nearby vanishing point is on the drawing table.

More complex perspectives sometimes require a centrolinead on each side, each adjusted and marked to avoid confusion. Sometimes a tall building needs three-point perspective, requiring a third centrolinead. Incidentally, it's advisable to color code the push pin hole locations with the drawing because the pins tend to pop out. Also, it makes it easier to return to this project if you're doing more than one rendering at a time.

Figure 2-3.   Perspective layout draftsman, Bill Grillo, at work.

After the building is drawn, cars, people, and trees can be added. For a rendering to be convincing, people and cars must be drawn to scale, which of course gives the building itself scale and reality. Specific car locations are decided using a sketch overlay, and scaled rectangles representing cars are drawn on the plan we're projecting from. The four corners of the cars are projected onto the perspective to get them placed in the picture in scale and in true direction of travel or angle if they are parked. With a 5-foot 6-inch horizon passing through the heads of adult people, they're in scale in the foreground or backgroundd (see Figure 2–1).

Transferring your Drawing to Illustration Board

Once the perspective is completed, one must decide where the borders should be. This determines the final size of the rendering itself. Some blueprinters have photocopy equipment that does enlargements or reductions on vellum or bond, if the original size isn't quite right.

Now we have the drawing, say 30″ × 17″, outlined on a sheet of tracing paper which is typically 36″ wide by 22″ high. The 33″ × 20″ illustration board, cut to size, is positioned under the drawing, which is still located in correct relationship to vanishing points and adjusted perspective T-square. The board is taped to the table and the transfer can start.

This is done by the *pounce* method, in which a 9H pencil is used to retrace the drawing, engraving it on the board underneath. The resulting fine grooves can be seen when a fluorescent desk lamp is held close. With grooves instead of lines, a sky wash can overlap the building, for example, without the outline of the building being lost, since the grooves still read through the paint. This technique works well for glass curtain walls, balconies silhouetted against the sky, and other elements. Cars and people are usually pounced after the building is rendered because it's easier to see them over the painted portion of the foreground.

Aerial views are usually projected from a site plan, whether a complex of buildings or a single structure. In order to get the best view, it's a good idea to build a crude model to place on the site plan to represent the massing. As in eye-level views, it is important to stay within the 60 degree cone of vision on the left and right sides and not to violate the vertical cone.

The cone of vision is simply what the human eye can see without turning one's head. Flies and rabbits can see within a very wide angle, but we are limited to a 60 degree angle in two dimensions, or a cone in three. So it is with perspective drawing. If one establishes a station point too close to a tall building or a long structure and constructs a perspective in violation of this rule, distortion will result.

Often, with a complex such as an office park it's advisable to move far enough away to achieve a telephoto effect. This makes all the buildings close to the same scale. Sometimes the original is done quite small and enlarged on vellum for reproduction. Also, the small perspective is easier to fax for client review.

The downtown Los Angeles office building shown in Figure 2–4 was developed by The Gerald Hines Interests. It was created from a multi-faceted plan and had more than the usual number of vanishing points. Since the architects had the project in the computer, we only had to decide on the angle and horizon height. The station point is high enough to show the street plan without compromising the dramatic effect of an eye-level view.

In the case of International Place in Boston (Figure 2–5), there were twenty-three vanishing points, mostly because the cylindrical towers were faceted, with each bay having its own vanishing points. Five or six centrolineads were needed to complete the perspective

Figure 2-4. Downtown Los Angeles office building developed by Gerald Hines Interests.

Figure 2-5. International Place, Boston, by Johnson & Burgee. There are twenty-three different vanishing points because the cylindrical towers don't have curved faces, but are faceted, and the rectangular elements have no common axis.

Figure 2-6. The line perspective (above) and rendering (below) show the International Place atrium, Boston. There are many vanishing points.

Figure 2-7. The completed rendering for the International Place atrium.

without having to make constant adjustments. The atrium of the same project also had many vanishing points (see Figures 2–6 and 2–7).

Interior perspectives are projected from floor plans using the same rules. Often one must view an interior space from outside in order to see enough, and to avoid distortion. This might mean, for example, creating a station point on the sidewalk to view the interior of a bank; the exterior walls would be left out. As in all eye-level views, I prefer the 5-foot 6-inch horizon for realism, and to keep people in scale easily.

Layout work in general involves situations that require you to improvise methods to achieve a result, but always within the general principles of perspective drawing. As long as the finished product is correct, and one hopes dramatic as well, we have achieved our objective.

3

Materials

■ After much experimentation I've developed a list of materials that give me the best results with a minimum of problems. For instance, I use tracing paper that is 100 percent rag bond since it pounces well with a minimum of tearing and is good for pencil sketches as well.

I use a made-to-order triple-thick 28″×42″ gray board which is cut to the size of each rendering. This thickness minimizes warping. I prefer gray over white board because it provides a better background for color applied to it.

The tempera paint itself must be permanent. In the past, certain brands of blue faded. This not only created big problems with skies, but greens and greys would get too warm over time, and this would totally change the rendering.

I've always worked with a limited palette of paints in two-ounce jars. I use several basic colors:

Dark Blue

Burnt Sienna

Yellow

Yellow Ochre

Spectrum Orange

Black

White

For accents I use

Magenta and Red

and occasionally

Phthalocyanine green and fluorescent colors.

The workhorse of the brushes is the Number 6 Liquitex Kolinsky Sable. It's expensive, but well worth it. Brush purchasing is no place to economize; cheaper brushes can cause you to waste time trying to do what only a good one can.

A new brush is best for very fine lines like butt-glazing at a distance. Slightly worn brushes are good for mullions or other thicker line work. An even older brush is good for striping brick, for example. Since I start a new brush about twice a month, they accumulate rapidly. The method I use to keep them classified is to date them when new, scratching the month and year on the tip with a push pin. Certain brushes become good for small scale brick or large scale brick, for example, and one remembers what number did what best. I haven't known other renderers to do this. I'm just sharing what has worked for me.

Flat, sable brushes are used for skies, walls, glass, ground surfaces, and water. For most foliage, I use a Number 5 round bristle brush as well as the Number 6 sable.

I don't ever use ruling pens for line work. The brush is more versatile, holds more paint and produces a better, less mechanical looking line. Also, it's easier to mix paint and adjust the mix with the brush you're using instead of transferring paint to a ruling pen. Of course, the brush is run against a straight edge held above the work for straight lines. Again, the straight edge is a 32-inch T-square without a head. After some years, the plastic edges lose their sharp corners, making the implement more comfortable to hold.

For mixing color in quantity for such elements as skies or entourage, I use an enameled steel butcher's tray. I use ceramic egg-crate-type palettes for smaller quantities. If I am interrupted, I can cover them to prevent the paints from drying out. Also, three shades of brick can be mixed separately side by side, for example. Some tempera renderers use the table itself as a palette, in larger and larger areas, until there's no clean space left. The table is then washed and they begin anew.

Remember to change the water in the jars often enough to avoid muddy colors. To add water when mixing paint, I use a small plastic squeeze bottle of clean water.

Although there are as many sets of beliefs on materials as there are artists, I hope my experience can be a good starting point for beginners on their way to learning what works best for them.

4

The Tempera Technique

■ Let's take a step-by-step walk through the development of a rendering of a downtown high-rise building: the U.S. Courthouse, Foley Square, New York City, Kohn Pedersen Fox Architects. I'll digress along the way to deal with other building types and situations.

We have a 450-foot-tall granite building on a small site surrounded by structures of medium height. The architects decided on a general view, which was represented by a photograph of the model that had been faxed to my office. At the initial meeting, we discussed other alternatives briefly. When we talked about the best *height* from which to view the building at the angle chosen, I recommended a 40-foot-high horizon rather than a 5-foot 6-inch eye-level horizon in order to see more of the site development.

Before beginning the projecting process, I had the typical floor plans and roof plan reduced to 1/16 scale to match the site plan. The site plan was situated on the layout table at about the angle that would result in the view of the model photo. Next, a very crude 1/16 scale model of the building was placed on the site plan to determine how far away our station point should be.

One must be careful to avoid "keystoning" of a high-rise perspective. Keystoning is the illusion of widening at the top; it results when the cone of vision rule is violated by getting too close. If I want to get closer than this rule allows, I can put some three-point perspective in the layout by using the perspective T-square at the base of the drawing to achieve some convergence in the vertical lines toward the sky. In this process, the arms of the T-square are adjusted in the opposite configuration from the usual one.

For this rendering, I decided against the three-point perspective and proceeded in the conventional way. I located the picture plane so as to result in a rendering that would be about 30 inches high. The various floor plans and the roof plan were placed successively over the site plan to project information on the corresponding facades. The footprints of the surrounding buildings were drawn around the site and projected on the layout in perspective using site photos to determine floor-to-floor dimensions and general appearance.

Prints were made during this process and faxed to the architects as the work went forward. When the line perspective was complete, we had a meeting to review facade details and discuss materials and color. After some minor refinements the drawing was pounced on the illustration board for painting (see Figure 4–1).

Figure 4-1. Line perspective,
U.S. Courthouse, Foley Square, New
York City.

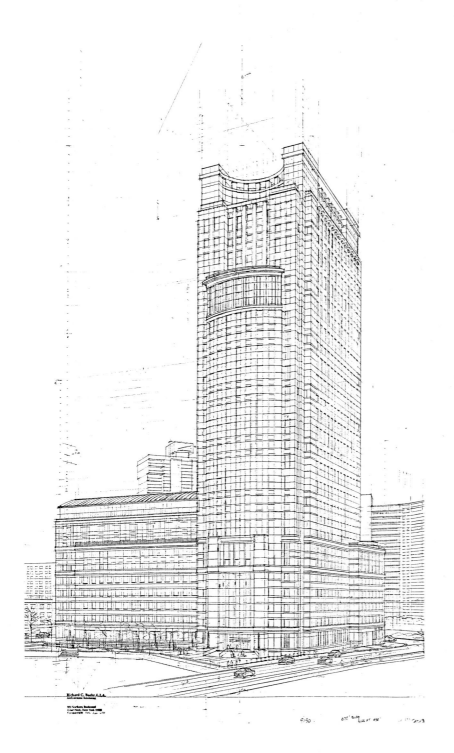

The project sponsor then requested a color study for further review. This shows the basic elements and their relationships to each other—the sky, the glass, and the stone face in both sun and shade. Sometimes I render a building with sunlight hitting all sides, but I felt this courthouse could be best shown with the contrast one achieves with a sunny side and a shade side. Color studies are not usually requested but you might find preparing one helps fine tune your color values. Because color renderings need to reproduce well in newsprint, you need to keep in mind what shades of grey your colors will assume.

In this category of tempera, the sky is the first area to be painted. I'm not a renderer who believes in illustrating buildings on rainy days. Although it's been said that we don't always have blue sky and low humidity, and for that reason all renderings need not depict ideal weather, I've never known how to break the news to a client that his or her building would be depicted in terrible weather. Most of my work has been commissioned by architects, developers, and ad agencies who want to "sell" a building or a space.

As a renderer you must decide how the tower will read against the sky. Because blue photographs lighter in black and white than its true value, the blue must be significantly darker in value than the building. Here, the building material for the courthouse is a light gray thermal granite. Therefore, a fairly typical blue sky can be rendered to be a darker value than that of the building's sunny side and still be lighter than in value than the shade side.

When the colors have been determined, the painting can begin. Following a sequence of steps is one key to creating a successful rendering.

I render the sky from the horizon up, inverting the rendering on the table. I use the following colors: dark blue, white, yellow, a little orange, and a very little black to soften the bright blue pigment. To have the even gradation from light to dark, I usually take the phone off the hook to allow me to do a continuous wash. I use a 1-inch flat sable brush and have plenty of paint in the butcher tray so I can proceed without pausing long to mix paint.

I almost always include clouds if only to be able to reflect them in the glass to enliven the reflection. Clouds also help to define the sky; they can be made to pass behind the building and not just surround the image. The clouds are made of white with blue and burnt sienna to avoid stark white—since "white" clouds aren't ever completely white. They are done

Figure 4-2. Color study, U.S. Courthouse, Foley Square, New York City.

Figure 4-3. The sky was rendered first, behind the building, then window glass with cloud and skyline reflections.

with a 3/4-inch flat brush held almost parallel to the surface with a side-to-side technique.

As you can see in the progress photos, with the line drawing engraved in the gray board, the sky wash can be freely run side to side without stopping at the edge of the building. The lines still read through where sky and building overlap.

Had this building been a dark granite, the sky would have a lighter value, perhaps overcast with some breaks of blue or blue with feathery cirrus cloud formations where needed to provide contrast for the building. Another option would be a pale, hazy, cloudless sky. This simple sky would also be a good choice for a building with very complex facade detailing, the sky providing some relief.

Once the sky is complete, I consider the glass in the building. In this case it's clear glass (not tinted) and thus will reflect the sky in many different ways but always a little darker and grayer than that portion of the sky being reflected. In general more light is reflected when the glass is seen at an angle, as on the shady side of this building. Glass seen head on is usually less reflective.

The best advice for learning how to render glass is get out there in the city and *look*. Try to translate what you see into a specific color and value in tempera, while keeping in mind that tempera is intrinsically flat and not "glassy." Good glass character can be achieved nonetheless. Having rendered buildings during the 60s, 70s, and 80s the "glassiest" of architectural decades so far, I found glass the most fascinating of all building materials to render. We've had mirror glass, solar bronze, solar gray, solex green, blue, black, copper, and burgundy glass and we've had some buildings with combinations—but they all reflect blue sky. (See, for example, Der Scutt's Revlon building, Figure 4–52.)

Back to Foley Square. Sequence is so important in rendering windows that I still sometimes use a checklist. After the initial wash, the next step is to portray clouds and distant reflections. Buildings that are far away will reflect grayer than closer ones. Closer, darker reflections are painted over that.

Of course, one must decide where these reflections belong in the composition. If a neighboring building has design or landmark significance, the reflection might have to be constructed in perspective. In these instances, you must be careful not to let the reflection become too important and disturb the rhythm and fabric of our building.

Because glass is never completely flat, reflections look more

Figure 4-4. Window jamb and head reflections, interior lighting and initial tones in granite areas are painted.

realistic if they are wavy. In a curtain wall notice how distortions occur near mullions and because of "oil canning." This is obviously not true of reflections in polished granite.

Mullion, window jamb, and window head reflections, are even darker. Now it's starting to look like glass. Check carefully to see that *all* the reflections are rendered since they're more difficult to put in later, out of sequence.

Next you will render interior lights—2×4 fluorescents or incandescent ceiling lighting or special lighting—whatever lights you would see from outside. Fluorescent lighting seen from outside helps to make the building look occupied and gives the facade depth and realism. Lighting is rendered after reflections because it penetrates them.

After lighting, the next elements rendered are drapery or blinds where the sun hits them. In the courthouse I showed drapery on the sunny side. Where mullions cross the window, they cast shadows on the drapery. Finally, the mullions themselves are rendered.

The facing of the courthouse is light gray thermal granite with black flecks. This stone was chosen to be compatible with the adjacent federal court buildings built in the 1920s. Looking at these buildings both up close and from a distance was helpful in deciding how to render the stone. I concluded that although we wouldn't see the flecks from our vantage point 672 feet away, the stone joints *would* read. I rendered the stone itself with subtle variations in color and value to express its character. In this building, the granite is almost uniform in color but I chose to exaggerate the variations to enliven the rendering.

The first stone surfaces to be painted are the window jambs, adjacent to the glass and, in this case, painted in shade. Because it's easier to establish the color and value of a material in shade after establishing the typical sunlit look, painting the three basic conditions—sun, shade, and shadow—on scrap board first can enhance confidence to forge ahead having "fine tuned" the values. You'll recall that the jamb reflections are already there (Figure 4–4).

The window returns can be rendered continuously up the facade as the reflection was, through the spandrels, which are painted later. On the sunlit side, the color of the returns is a warm gray reflecting nearby sunlit surfaces. On the shade side, the returns are a darker cool gray, and the facade is a lighter warm gray, catching reflected sunlight from surrounding buildings and street.

After the window and column returns were painted, the face itself

Figure 4-7. Site elements, cars, people and trees are rendered.

Figure 4-8. Glasswork and reflections.   **Figure 4-9.** Addition of mullions and brickwork.

Figure 4-10. Granite front and glass canopy added.   **Figure 4-11.** Trees and plantings.

The facade was then extended down to the base. Figure 4–10 through 4–13 show the final touches on the facade and entrance. Some sidewalk is reflected in the underside of the canopy. In Figures 4–11 and 4–12 trees and people were added to show activity and give scale to the building.

Figure 4-12. Finished rendering 345 Hudson Street. Architect: Berg and Forster.

The Aerial View

For this category I'll discuss my rendering of a high-rise apartment complex by Costas Kondylis, architects. Again, I like to make some crude models of the buildings at the scale of the site plans to help decide the best view. As in the case of the office tower, we must be sure not to violate the cone-of-vision rule. (See Figure 4–13.)

Typically, the height or horizon established in the perspective should result in a balance between seeing enough of the site and not too much of the roofs. In this rendering, the buildings are on a site in New Jersey high above the nearby Hudson River, which we want to see, along with Manhattan, in the background. Of course, for good composition we never want to split the building in half with the horizon. Similarly, the horizontal angle chosen should enhance the architectural design and highlight the entrance elements. As with the height study, the 60° cone of vision must include everything

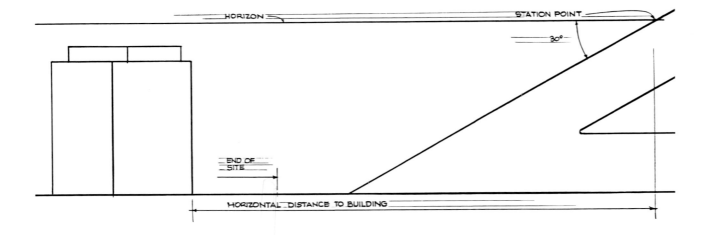

Figure 4–13. Model is viewed from horizon height of 192 feet using a 30°–60° triangle to locate a station point back far enough to avoid distortion.

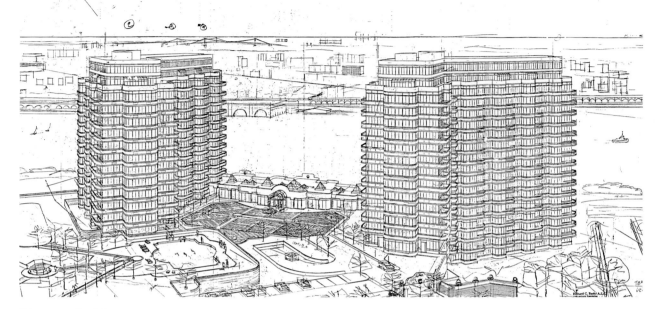

Figure 4-14. Completed line perspective. Carlyle Towers, New Jersey.

Figure 4-15. Sky wash, river background, and beginning elements.

Figure 4-16. Refinement of the glass.

we want in the rendering. Establishing the view is a process that can take an hour or more.

After the view is established, we can decide on the size of the perspective drawing by moving the picture plane back and forth and doing some quick projections. It's sometimes easier to work small and enlarge the completed projection to final size before pouncing it (see Figure 4–14). The sky and river behind the buildings were rendered first, then the glass and facade, using the same general sequence as in the Foley Square rendering.

With the site itself, the parking area is rendered first. Some renderers render blacktop very dark, since it is the color of new paving. This, however, makes the overall rendering too dark. Also, the color of asphalt pavement lightens as the tar binder wears from the surface and the aggregate is exposed. I always render blacktop lighter than the adjacent grass areas and darker than concrete walks.

In all rendering, color and values are relative. Therefore, the first paint on the board is the hardest to get exactly right because there's nothing there for it to relate to. For the gray paving, I mix blue, burnt sienna, and white with some orange and yellow ochre. Subtle variations add interest and reflect the real world. Similarly, the grass areas are given natural variations in color and value.

Figure 4-17. Buildings completed and site elements developed.

Figure 4-18. Finished rendering.

Figure 4-19. Recreation center, Teheran. Architect: David Chang; Developer: William Levitt.

Figure 4-20. Theoretical site Heavy Ion Fusion Center. Designed by Brookhaven National Laboratory.

Figure 4-21. Hauppauge office park, NY. Architect: Mojo Stumer.

The foreground was rendered with cloud shadows, which help to make the buildings more sunny and bright. The distant background was added with soft, muted tones to keep it where it belongs and to help "pop" the contrasty apartment towers in our project.

Figure 4–19 was designed as part of a residential development in Teheran, Iran to be built by William Levitt at the time of the Shah's regime. Political changes ended the project in the planning stages. Sunlight in the rendering is concentrated in the pool area, with less intense light on soccer activity and parking areas.

The Heavy Ion Fusion Center rendering was commissioned by Brookhaven National Laboratory to illustrate a design for a proto-type of a nuclear fusion power generating station.

The science of this project is fascinating. Very briefly, the site consists of underground tunnels containing tubes that penetrate super-conducting magnets. Inside these tubes, the atomic particles are accelerated. The particles travel from three linear accelerators, seen on the outer square, to the holding rings from where they are stored then diverted to the center complex from opposite directions, colliding in a fusion reaction. The resulting heat is converted to electric power and sent out to the power grid.

The Hauppauge office park provided another challenge in per-spective. The viewpoint had to be high enough to show some of the building in the rear without showing too much roof area.

Interiors

In my experience, interior renderings present more of a challenge than those of exteriors for one reason—light. Outside, the sun is a given, and it can usually be moved around from Northwest to Northeast if necessary and even taken from due north if the client insists it's not relevant. Therefore, the sun can be located where it will produce the most dramatic visual effects. With interiors, however, daylight and artificial light are integral to the architecture and cannot be altered greatly.

In the elevator lobby rendering of 1450 Broadway, Max Gordon and Associates, architects, the lighting is an integral part of the design. There is indirect ceiling lighting, downlighting over brushed stainless wall panels with lighting strips in them, and a backlit polished stainless element on the end wall. The glow behind this metal

Figure 4-22. Office building lobby 1450 Broadway, New York, NY. Mirrored walls always present challenges, the main one being that one hopes what gets reflected is something we want to see. Architect: Max Gordon and Associates.

Figure 4-23. Lobby, 1450 Broadway, New York City, Max Gordon & Associates, architects.

feature was airbrushed. The polished marble floor, although very dark in color, still reflects what's going on or it wouldn't look polished. The lady in this rendering was lifted from a Lord & Taylor ad, complete with shopping bag.

Often with interior images, the natural boundaries of the drawings don't lend themselves to rectangular matting. In these cases I leave the rendering edges rough—a style called a vignette. This can

Figure 4-24. New York overnight quarters for an international airline. Interior design: Hertzfeld Design.

also minimize potential distortion of complicated interiors. The bar in Figure 4–24 was part of a eight-sided room designed for an international airline. The vignette worked well to show off its features.

The original lobby design for the Revlon building was a three-story scheme, with escalators to the second floor retail area. It was later scaled back for cost reasons. A view like this must be taken from outside the space in order to see everything. The cutaway was the only way to show all the elements without distortion.

The recessed ceiling fixtures bathe the floor and walls with light, but the white ceiling only receives reflected light and is rendered warm grey. The shadows on the column elements are exaggerated to highlight the design.

In this daytime rendering of Edward Larrabee Barnes's lobby at 599 Lexington Avenue (Figure 4–26), light coming through the glass wall overpowers interior lighting. Photos were taken at the

Figure 4-25. Revlon building entrance interior. Architect: Der Scutt.

Figure 4-26. Lobby, 599 Lexington Avenue, New York City. Edward Larrabee Barnes, John Ming-Yee Lee, Architects.

construction site to establish what exterior objects we would see from inside. The outside scene is much brighter than the inside one and was rendered first. The glass wasn't rendered except for the structural glass

Figure 4-27. The goal in this rehabilitated Kuwaiti Parliament building by HOK was to achieve a feeling of dignity and serenity. This was helped by the uplighting that illuminated the ceiling from the hollow columns and their bases.

elements that were done with a phthalo green transparent wash. Glass edges and butt joints were rendered as lines, with the stainless steel components added last. The marble walls, although not highly reflective, do reflect ceiling lighting and high contrasts in the floor surface. The highly polished floor reflects people, columns, and other objects.

Figure 4-28. Entrance view, Kuwaiti Parliament Building.

The rendering of the entrance to the Kuwaiti Parliament building rehabilitation by HOK has light coming from three sources: sunlight from the right, reflected sun from the left, and some uplighting inside the column elements. (See Figure 4–28.) In addition, daylight is coming through the other entrance at the other end of the building. This results in a glow in the space and shadows only on the sunny side. The glass entry has some vague reflections, with the distant entry daylight penetrating them.

Photomontage

In what is currently being called photomontage, typically a proposed building is rendered directly on a large color photograph of an urban site, this being easier than rendering the entire city with the new building in place. Robert Schwartz acquired a reputation for such work in the 1950s and 1960s. His aerial tempera renderings of New York City and Boston were filled with fascinating detail.

The photomontage method saves time, but it does have some disadvantages. The photos ordered for the job have to meet many requirements. First, the shoot has to be scheduled for a clear day, for which you can wait weeks. The angle and altitude the photographer takes must be specific and chosen for the best view of the new building. There are other problems. In New York City flight clearances close to Manhattan are not automatic since LaGuardia and Newark airports are so close. If it's winter, special care needs to be taken because the sun angle is always too low to be ideal—even at noon.

The photo used to create the World Financial Center montage was taken in March and had less than ideal light to work with. After the 40-inch-wide photo was dry-mounted on foam core, it was overlaid with mylar which is more transparent than paper, and allows you to see as much as possible of the photo underneath. The vanishing points and scale of the site and adjacent buildings were established. The new architecture could then be constructed in line perspective in scale with the downtown skyline. With all these formidable tasks to complete, at least one doesn't have to be concerned about finding the best view, since it's a given (see Figure 4–29).

Transferring the line drawing to the photo can be the most mind-bending phase of this process. When you pounce a drawing onto blank illustration board, it can be seen easily, but on a photo of a city, these small grooves can get lost. For example, after one wash for the glass areas, the lines are lost and must be pounced again. In addition, the "temperature" of the photo must be respected and the building rendered cool or warm to match it.

When the finished work is photographed, the difference in reflective quality between the painted area and the matte-finish photo will disappear. Since we are photographing a photograph, the original photo must be bright and contrasty, not dark and murky, to be able to survive a second generation. The rendering of the World Financial Center, Figure 4–30, was enlarged to cover an entire wall at Olympia & York's midtown sales office.

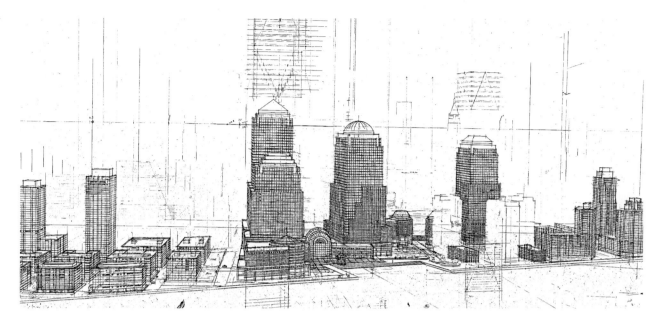

Figure 4-29. Line perspective, World Financial Center, New York City. Cesar Pelli & Associates, architetects.

Figure 4-30. Finished rendering. World Financial Center, New York City. Project was rendered on a 40′ matte finish photo mounted on foam core. Housing elements to the left and right of the project were "ad libbed", not having been designed at the time.

Figure 4-31. London Bridge City, London. Architect: Johnson & Burgee. The Royal Navy cruiser is a permanent neighbor, functioning as a war museum.

When the city of London asked for a rendering of London Bridge City in the context of its surroundings, painting the new project on a photograph was the best option. The photo is very "cool" with hazy sunlight coming from beyond the buildings—not what one would choose. This meant that the major surfaces on the rendered structures would be in shade. To enhance the new buildings, they were rendered in tones warmer than their surroundings with some reflected "glow" from the sunny surfaces adjacent.

In the case of International Place in Boston, John Burgee was asked to show how one tower, Phase II, would look in the skyline alongside the existing Phase I (Figure 4–32). The contrast in this winter photo worked out to the advantage of the new building. A successful photomontage rendering should cause people to ask, "Which is the new building?" as this one does.

Winter light also proved successful to show off Jung Brannen's One Lincoln Street in Boston. The sun angle was good for high-lighting the new building (center). Careful planning can produce good photos for photomontage even in low light.

With Johnson & Burgee's 343 Sansome Street in San Francisco, the city required several renderings in order to judge the new building's appearance in the context of the neighborhood. As photomontage assures us that the existing elements are exactly as we see them, it was the ideal method for the task.

The bird's-eye view needed to show the building's aerial profile fitting in, if not enhancing, the skyline. The photo supplied had unusual characteristics to work with: lavender tint, and late after-

Figure 4-32. International Place, Boston. Architect: Johnson & Burgee. The two towers are the only cylindrical buildings shown; Phase II has a conical roof.

Figure 4-33. One Lincoln Street, Boston. Designed by Jung Brannen, Architects.

Figure 4-34. Aerial view 343 Sansome Street, San Francisco.

noon sun. The building (center) was rendered in similar subdued tones—to blend in, not stand out.

The bright photograph of the front of the building was ideal for photomontage. The glancing sun helped to highlight Philip Johnson's facade detail (Figure 4–35). In order to enhance the photorealism of the presentation, I carefully painted around the parked car located in the original photo. Rendered cars can rarely be as realistic as those photographed, especially at this scale.

The rear view photomontage of 343 Sansome Street is almost all new rendering, but there's enough of the photo left to place the building in its proper context. The sun direction worked perfectly for accenting the new outdoor cafe.

Figure 4-35. Front view 343 Sansome Street, San Francisco.

Figure 4-36. Rear view 343 Sansome Street, San Francisco. The adjacent building in the shade as well as the distant hazy structures are both part of the original photo.

Rendering Water

Water always enhances an architectural rendering and the way it is rendered tells a story about that environment.

Although water can be rendered in many ways, I usually use a graded wash, even for small areas. The general principle is to render the water lighter toward the horizon and darker toward the foreground, as it reflects the sky. The amount of color gradation varies with the size of the body of water, the angle of the perspective, and weather conditions. Water can change color dramatically depending primarily on the sky and wind conditions.

Water begins to look realistic when the reflections are added. Water is always surrounded by objects of some kind, usually determined in the architectural plans.

Figure 4-37. Epcot Center Hotel, Orlando, FL. Architects: Brennan Beer Gorman.

Figure 4-38. The Galaxy, Guttenberg, NJ. The rendering of these buildings, located on the Palisades, was similar in approach and execution to that of Carlyle Towers. The skyline was rendered with it's well-known skyscrapers to show off it's view of New York. Architect: The Gruzen Partnership; Project Architect: Peter Samton.

Waves are done after the reflections are rendered. To create water texture or minor wave activity, I use a flat 3/4-inch brush, fairly dry, held at a low angle, moving side to side. You must add waves in certain instances, for instance, if sailboats appear to be moving, the water cannot be glassy smooth. In the Epcot Center Hotel rendering, the water was rendered mirror-smooth to emphasize the tranquility of the environment.

The Hudson river in Figure 4–38 was rendered as it would look with light variable winds, with waves too small to read at this distance and dark streaks where gusts produce local disturbances. With more wind, skyline and boats couldn't be reflected, less wind and sailboats wouldn't be sailing. The *value* of the water had to contrast with both the sunny and shade side of the towers.

Rendering Glass

If all architects had to name one building material that is the most versatile, variable, and limitless from the visual aspect, it would have to be glass. With the introduction and wide use of reflective glass, tinted glass, and countless combinations of glass coatings, architects have gained a whole new vocabulary of expression in the last 30 years.

The oil crisis of the 70s intensified the drive toward conservation of energy, creating incentives for greater use of heat-reflective windows, and encouraged architects to use reflective and heat-absorbing tinted glass. This resulted in a new look in modern architecture.

Naturally, architectural renderers were challenged to illustrate this new glass at its exciting best. This material, more than any other, changes in appearance according to the weather, time of day, season, and what's going on around it, inside and out.

The green reflective glass of the Newport Office Center in Jersey City, with its flush precast spandrels (Figure 4–39), is the key component of this slick office tower typical of its time. It reflects a blue sky, rendered darker at the top of the building with the values becoming gradually lighter going down, always being a darker value than what is being reflected, at least at this angle.

Distant reflections are lighter than those nearby. To accent the corner, building reflections are at different heights. On the shade side, care must be taken to keep the values of the glass and spandrels different, for clarity—in the color rendering, and for black and white reproductions.

In the Garden City Center at Mitchell Field, Long Island, the clear reflective glass simply reflects everything, allowing none of the interior to read through it. Sky reflections in glass follow the same color gradation as the sky: they brighten the closer they come to the source of sunlight.

The New York office building (Figure 4–41) features three types of glass, clear vision glass, grey spandrel glass, and reflective glass. Notice how the intensity of reflections vary in each case. In the red granite building, note the different reflective properties of glass and polished stone. This opaque material shows both shadows and reflections.

The Bronx New York medical office building in Figure 4–43 has green reflective glass on both the windows and spandrels of the office floors with a combination of dark and white mullions.

Figure 4-39. Newport Office Center, NJ. Architect: Leo Kornblath
Associates P.C.

Figure 4-40. Garden City Center, Long Island, NY. Architect and
Developer: Rodolitz Associates.

Figure 4-41. Photograph of glass reflections in an office building.

Figure 4-42. Photograph of reflections and shadows from the adjoining buildings.

Figure 4-43. Medical office building, Bronx, NY. Newman and Novak, Architects.

The sun does not cast shadows on clean glass, but it does cast them on the white mullions. These images have to be planned so that the reflections can be rendered in the adjacent glass surface before the mullions are rendered in that face.

The slight distortion in the reflected images is necessary, as mentioned before, because glass is never completely flat—as long as they are not as extreme as in Figure 4-52.

The reflections in the perpendicular glass surfaces are darker than what they're reflecting; this provides the necessary contrast in values where the two meet in the corner. The white mullion reflections are also darker than what *they* are reflecting. All of these reflections must be rendered before the actual mullion grids are added.

Figure 4-44. Winter Garden, Battery Park City, New York, NY. Architect: Cesar Pelli and Associates.

The clear glass of the lobby with its metal buttons doesn't reflect as much as the mirror glass, especially the areas close to the ground where there are no sky reflections. Some semi-transparent highlights are applied as a thin wash with a flat brush, before butt joints or buttons are rendered.

The photograph of Cesar Pelli's Winter Garden at the World Trade Center, shows how the reflective quality of the glass changes with the angle of the glass. One flat portion of the facade reflects a very bright western sky. The white canvas umbrellas inside penetrate the reflections with varying success, according to the brightness of the reflections.

In the Two Wall Street rendering only interior lighting and sunlit drapery are bright enough to be seen.

Figure 4-45. Two Wall Street, New York, NY.

Figure 4-46. New York City office building.

The 4 P.M. Saturday photo of a New York office building (Figure 4–46) illustrates how little interior can be seen when outside light is so much stronger than interior lighting. It's almost all exterior reflection except for the lone coffee drinker on the left.

The entrance interior for the office building on the Meirendorfplatz in Berlin, has daylight coming in front and rear, plus interior lighting. The interior was rendered even lighter to exaggerate the openness of the space. The difference in reflective qualities of the clear glass and the blue reflective glass are exaggerated to emphasize the lobby interior—the view through the garden beyond. The granite is thermal finish which diffuses sunlight; the stainless steel is satin finish.

This Lexington Avenue (Figure 4–48) facade illustrates how

Figure 4-47. Mierendorfplatz, Berlin.

Figure 4-48. Lexington Avenue office building.

Figure 4-49. World Financial Center, Battery Park City, NY.

Figure 4-50. Office building, Long Island, NY. Shows a variety of colored glass.

clear glass and colored spandrel glass reflect the same objects with different values, but reflect the bright sky at a glancing angle similarly. The rendering of the Long Island office building (Figure 4–50) has almost identical glass types. Note how reflections are similar on the right side.

This World Financial Center building entrance element has clear window glass, reflective spandrel glass, and blue spandrel glass, all handling light and reflections in different ways. Compare these reflective patterns with those of the Revlon Building (Figure 4–52) with its different kinds of reflective glass: burgundy, copper, and black. All glass reflects the sky and buildings differently as do the glass types in the photograph.

Figure 4-51. New York office building, 900 Third Avenue. This photograph shows distorted reflections that would need to be minimized in a rendering. See Chapter 6 for the *rendering* of 900 Third Avenue.

The view of 900 Third Avenue shows how reflections in the real world can be too distorted for a rendering. What is being reflected can be just too busy, as was the case with the Revlon building.

Architect Der Scutt was commissioned to design a new facade and lobby for a typical 1960s white brick office building on Madison Avenue in New York City. For the outside, he designed a new curtain wall consisting of reflecting glass of burgundy copper color, and black, all reflecting blue sky and adjacent buildings.

In this case, the building opposite is the General Motors Building, which has marble columns and dark windows with spandrel panels between them. To reflect vertical stripes in our multicolored glass facade would make the rendering too busy. Instead, the reflections were designed to enhance the new glass wall without departing from a typical Manhattan skyline impression.

Figure 4-52. Revlon building, New York. Der Scutt Architect.

Having decided upon the pattern and placement of reflections, we then determined what *colors* to render the glass. With the actual burgundy, copper, and black glass samples on the office windowsill, we could see how blue sky would make them appear. A color study of a small portion of the facade was rendered and shown to the architect along with the line perspective. Minor corrections were made, and the color work went forward.

Contrast and Color Values

Colors and values are the language of rendering expression, and the tempera medium provides a full vocabulary of expression for them. It is uniquely suited for creation of a full range of values with all their nuances and subtleties.

To refine an understanding of values, a beginning renderer should start thinking in terms of the ten shades of gray from white to black. It's a good experience to draw a chart resembling a ladder, and, using a graphite or wax-based pencil on mylar or paper, fill in values from one to ten. Then, experimenting with paint, judge what values various colors are. This is pretty basic stuff, but it must become second nature to know instinctively how a color rendering will reproduce in black and white. A rendering has to be pretty strong to survive reproduction in a newspaper.

A general comment about color values: Many professional renderings don't have a full range. The value scale ranges from zero to ten—with zero being white and ten being black. Some renderings use values only from zero to five or six. To me, this is comparable to using half the notes on a piano. (The watercolor readers may now be making faces.) It's not that I don't appreciate a soft and subtle watercolor rendering. For depicting a building on a peaceful spring afternoon, watercolor is delightful. However, when a rendering has a marketing purpose (for an owner, buyer, tenant, philanthropist, or end user) I want to use *all* the notes. You want to always be thinking about values for a newspaper reproduction with *punch*.

The black and white reproduction of the color rendering on opposite page reproduced well for newspaper advertising. The sky was rendered dark because blue often reproduces lighter than its true value. This off-white building was easier to render with contrasting values than a dark building for obvious reasons.

Figure 4-53. Residential condominiums. Architect: Mojo Stumer.

Figure 4-54. Residential condominiums. Black and white reproduction understates the value of the blue sky. Architect: Mojo Stumer.

Figure 4-55. This rendering was used as a color study to decide on white brick and green copper versus tan brick and bronze.

5

Office Practice

■ One doesn't remember many quotes verbatim from architecture school but I recall one worth repeating here. At the University of Cincinnati School of Architecture one seminar speaker was the head of the design studio of the Chrysler Corporation. He said, "Set yourself up right." He meant make your office arrangement ideal and efficient for what you'll be doing there for the next forty years. I have never compromised on this.

I favor large, flat surfaces, not small drawingboards. For tables, we have 6′8″ × 3′ solid-core doors with plastic board cover, two Luxo flourescents per table—each having one cool white and one daylight tube for color balance. (We use incandescents on the layout tables.)

The windows facing northeast are wall to wall from countertop to ceiling. Other walls are covered with cork or homasote so drawings can be put up for instant reference; this minimizes shuffling through pages of prints. The floor is covered with resilient tile which allows the drafting chairs on casters to move easily.

The sound system is very important. I can't imagine rendering all these years without good radio to occupy that portion of the brain that's available while rendering. With 80+ stations in the New York Metropolitan area including National Public Radio there's usually good talk available. The stereo speakers are ceiling mounted, aimed at where my ears are while I'm working. Good jazz, classical, or talk is a wonderful complement to architectural rendering. Another essential is a telephone headset. Certain phases of rendering can be done while talking on the phone and the headset frees up one's hands. If I want to make a 20-minute call to a friend or relative, I wait until the rendering needs something I can do while I'm on the phone.

Of course, the fax machine is essential for receiving information and sending sketches for approval. I still marvel at faxing a sketch to Europe after 6 P.M. (lower rates) with specific questions. At 9 A.M. the next morning, 3 P.M. European time, they have had most of the day to get the questions answered, and we can proceed without waiting. Airmail takes one week or more—Federal Express, two to three days.

As far as staff is concerned, I have a layout person in his own private office with his own sound system and his own choice of audio material. You may be wondering, what's all this talk about radio? It's especially helpful when you spend a straight weekend of work in an empty building; you can let Thelonius Monk or Count Basie fill the place, as we did in architecture school.

Regarding office operation, the simpler the better. I'm not a believer in written contracts unless required by the client. Renderer friends who do seem to have no fewer problems collecting fees than I do with handshake deals. Consequently, I have never had a secretary, preferring to use freelance people for proposals and occasional correspondence. The majority of clients are architects and large developers who honor their commitments. Small developers are usually on a C.O.D. basis, reflecting their sometimes slightly different standards of ethics.

For more mundane details of record keeping I use the common numbering system for rendering jobs, for instance, 9501, with the first two digits indicating the year, for later reference. Line perspectives and 35mm slides are filed accordingly. The active drawing file goes back six to nine years, and older ones to the archives. I can retrieve any perspective to update a rendering if a previously rendered building has undergone alteration or addition and a new rendering is needed. I keep a record book containing client name, project description, fee, layout and rendering time in hours, and date billed and date paid. Time records for past renderings are useful in setting fees for new work, especially when you are bidding for the job and do not want to overestimate the hours involved. My tendency is to be optimistic and underestimate time required—this is equally problematic.

Some renderers grant the client reproduction rights and retain the original drawing or painting. Again, in the interest of simplicity, my clients get the original rendering after it's been photographed in 35mm color in the office.

One of the appeals of a rendering practice as compared to architecture is how "clean" it is. You get an assignment, do the work, ship or deliver the rendering, and get paid. The assignments are scheduled, and typically several jobs are in progress at any given time. I try to stay flexible to be able to accommodate rush projects and to avoid turning away work, although this hasn't always worked. In 1985, perhaps the peak of the frothy 80s, we had to refuse 56 renderings, since we were chronically overbooked and then some.

The main appeal of rendering for me is the infinite variety of projects I get to work on for a wide variety of creative people. Each rendering is a challenge not just to complete but to illustrate the design in the best possible way. It's really satisfying to inject excitement into a meeting of architects and real estate or advertising people with a rendering. As a major player once said, "It sings."

6

Retrospective

■ I often think of the choice I made in being a renderer and not a practicing architect. Sometimes I see an architect who has worked on one hospital rehabilitation and/or addition for six years because the project is large and complex, and I'm thankful for the great variety of people and projects that I regularly become involved in. This retrospective attempts to represent the spectrum of my work.

Donald Trump's original proposal for what is now called Riverside South was a design by Helmut Jahn called Television City. The client required that the rendering show the project, and, most important, its relationship to New York City. We decided on the best view for the new buildings and ordered aerial photographs to be taken from that location. An altitude of 600 feet was chosen in order to show the landscaped site and to avoid splitting the 70-story residential towers and the 150-story central structure in half with the horizon.

The pilot and photographer were given the desired angle and altitude, but taking photographs of a site from an aircraft is difficult at 120 miles per hour in choppy air . They made several passes, then sent some 8 × 10s from which to select. A 40-inch-wide cronoflex was made from the best one. Using a print of this photo to trace over, a line perspective was started.

Since there is nothing more authentic than a photograph, Manhattan's buildings could then be drawn in at their precise locations and scale. The one exception, the Empire State Building, was moved several blocks north in order to include it in the picture.

Concurrently with the background work, the site plan was placed on the table at the right distance and angle, and the new buildings were drawn, using the 600-foot horizon.

The site plan was then transferred to the board for painting. The first basic decision to be made was should the new buildings be darker or lighter than the background? The casual reader looking at a two- or three-column-wide newspaper reproduction should know quickly which buildings are the new ones. After we decided on darker buildings because they are mostly glass, rendering began with a light sky. Next, some preliminary background values were placed to establish the general value range. The new buildings were started,

Figure 6-1. Television City—Riverside South, New York City.
Murphy/Jahn Architects.

glass first, following the same painting sequence as shown in
Chapter 4.

To show the potential development of vacant David's Island in
Long Island Sound, the Gruzen Partnership office did a six-week
design study. The rendering had to depict a prototype for a community that would later have more extensive planning and design work.
Then, after initial acceptance was achieved, the planning would go
forward.

These are residential buildings with light tan brick, calling for a
darker background. After they were projected in the usual way and
transferred to the board, the water was rendered first, behind the
buildings. Next, the site was painted bright and sunny, paved areas
first, then grass, then walks. Walks in a bird's-eye rendering are a
case in which an older less-pointed brush can often be used with a
single stroke for the five-foot-wide walk.

Figure 6-2. David's Island, Long Island Sound, New York. Architect: The Gruzen Partnership.

For aerial renderings, one must choose a sun angle that is possible with the site orientation and that will provide the most dramatic presentation. After this angle is chosen, a line on the site is drawn and its vanishing point on the horizon located. This is usually "off the table," and the perspective T-square is employed to line up with the line and the horizon so that a number of these "light lines" as we call them, can be drawn on the site. Then, any shadows cast will be parallel in plan but vanishing to a point on the horizon as they would in perspective. This is especially important if there are a number of tall buildings on a large site. Again, we're always working with sequence in mind, rendering the site behind the buildings first, then the buildings on top. This sequence assumes the renderer has the image of the final result in mind as he or she proceeds.

Brookhaven National Laboratory's particle accelerator operates on similar scientific principles to those driving the Heavy Ion Fusion

Figure 6-3. The developer's goal for this rendering was to attract a corporation from a central city location to this building. We decided to emphasize the placid environment and country air of the Connecticut site. Architect: Alexander Cooper & Associates.

Reactor (page 38). The scientific aspects of this "machine" as it's called by physicists are also worth an explanation.

Among the existing buildings in the background are the LINAC, or linear accelerator and the alternating gradient synchotron or AGS. At this complex, atomic particles are accelerated by a series of electromagnets then "stored" at their ultimate velocity in the AGS ring. The steel tubes containing these speeding particles are surrounded by electromagnets.

Next the particles are diverted in tunnels tangential to the ring where they will collide with "targets" or enter the bubble chamber—in controlled experiments designed to learn more about the nature of matter. The LINAC and AGS were to be used to inject the particles into the large ring dubbed ISABELLE.

Figure 6-4. Brookhaven National Laboratory wanted to "sell" Isabelle, a state-of-the-art particle accelerator to the local community on Long Island, the New York State Department of Energy, and the political establishment. A rendering was needed to show this vast underground tunnel in the form of a ring, with its connection to the existing linear accelerator and its relationship (and comparative size) to the laboratory complex beyond.

This ring was planned as an underground tunnel 2½ miles in circumference through which particles would travel in two vacuum tubes in opposite directions. They were to be propelled along by a series of superconducting electromagnets around the tubes. For maximum efficiency, the magnets would be supercooled to almost absolute zero (−452°F) by liquid helium at which temperature the electrical resistance in the magnets is very low. The tubes in the ISABELLE ring, would pass through separate "halls" where experiments could be performed.

Hadron Hall (Figure 6–5), is one such facility on the ring. Notice the two tubes, cutaway at left, through which the particles are moving in opposite directions. Beyond the monitoring machine with its

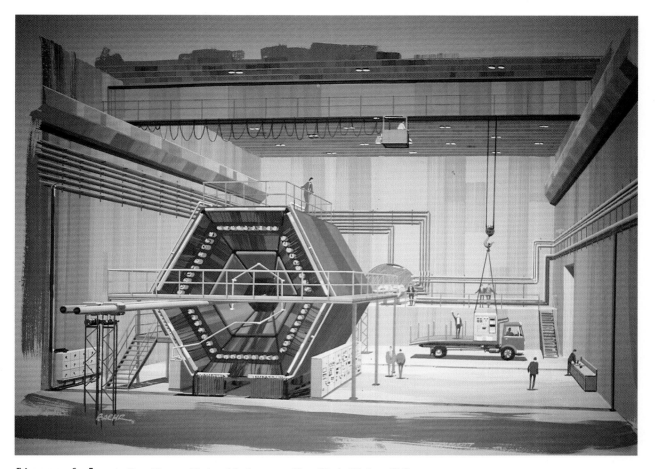

Figure 6-5. At Brookhaven National Laboratory, New York, Hadron Hall is an underground chamber in the Isabelle ring (Figure 6–6) through which the particles pass and are monitored.

instrument panel is the continuation of the tunnel though which the tubes pass.

Whatever particles were not stopped by fixed targets or generic particle detectors would finally hit concrete beam stops and be absorbed, resulting in low-level radiation in the concrete.

The Howard Savings Bank headquarters building was designed by the Grad Partnership. The background and foreground in the rendering are subdued with cloud shadows to enhance the sunny quality of our project. With this precast concrete structure, we can easily picture what the building will look like in bright sunlight.

As in every tempera rendering, the very first paint applied to the blank gray illustration board is the most tentative. Here, the roof sur-

Figure 6-6. High rise condominium residence, New Jersey Shore.

Figure 6-7.   The Howard Savings Bank headquarters. Architect: The Grad Partnership.

faces were done first. The site and roof surface could be rendered different ways. I never care what color the real roof will be—black or white—I do what's best for the rendering. A flat roof won't even be seen after the building is built.

Usually light gray is the best color. Here, that value contrasts well with the facade and has a sunny quality. This shade of gray was selected with the viewpoint in mind to express the plane of the roof and to avoid monotony. Next, the sunnier grass areas with the drives and walks on top of that were done.

The glass areas of the building were painted in the usual sequence of reflections, drapery, mullions, and so on, to keep everything in balance. I like to do a little of the dark foreground and background as the rendering progresses to keep the value and color relationship correct, rather than finish the building completely before painting the surrounding land.

The Amerada Hess Corporation had eight 34,000-ton oil barges built in South Korea. Some were to be used at their St. Croix Virgin Islands refinery, but some were to be leased or sold. The company wanted to produce a marketing brochure and took photos of the vessels doing all their various jobs—except for taking crude oil directly from an offshore platform. For this they wanted a photo-realistic rendering to go in the centerfold.

Figure 6-8. The crude from offshore oil platforms is stored in a moored underwater tank (brown color) with above-water crew facilities and helicopter pad. Empty tankers are met by a small boat with a hose from the facility for loading the oil onto the tanker. The transparency of the water was exaggerated to tell the story.

As with building renderings, the plans of the naval architect were used for drawing the barge. The offshore rig was researched and the image gleaned from industry periodicals.

Again the basics: How are we going to be sure the offshore rig and the barge will both read against the water? The barge deck color is a "given"—that characteristic dull marine red intended perhaps to blend with the inevitable rust conditions at sea. The hull of the barge is black, close to the value of the water, but a white wake at the waterline helps to separate them. Highlights on a black surface can be almost white. One does what works for the picture. I always prefer to make the subject *bright* against a dark background, so the water was rendered dark and the barge deck a bleached, sundrenched version of the dull red color. Tugboats come in all sizes: therefore, I used crew members to indicate the scale of the vessel.

The rendering of New York City's Williamsburg Bridge was required to illustrate the proposed added lanes and to show the upgrading of existing lanes to meet federal standards. This perspec-

Figure 6-9. Amerada Hess Corporation oil barge.

tive was done *not* from a photograph, but by projecting from a plan of the bridge.

When you are used to plans of buildings, a bridge 100 feet wide and 1.5 miles long becomes a perspective challenge. To prevent the distant tower from disappearing completely, I worked from a small-scale plan placed relatively far away from the station point to achieve a slight telephoto effect. The intricate structural steel towers were both fun and a challenge to draw correctly. Authenticity is essential with an existing structure familiar to New Yorkers.

In rendering the towers, the steel members further away were rendered first as silhouetted against the sky. The steel surfaces receiving reflected light were rendered next, and, finally, the sunlit surfaces were rendered. Then the shadows of the suspended cables and wires were painted on the steel, followed by the tension members themselves.

Having done Levitt rendering for 16 years, I was current in my knowledge of the changing tastes of the American and foreign home buyers. We did projects on Long Island, in New Jersey, Pennsylvania, Maryland, Virginia, Michigan, Illinois, Florida,

Figure 6-10. The specially designed tug in Figure 6–10 was rendered for a presentation to the board of directors of the Amerada Hess Corporation; it was also used in their annual report. It's an oversized tug designed to push oversized oil barges. The high wheelhouse allows the captain to see over the empty barge being pushed. At the eye level used, the lighter water near the horizon reflects the lighter sky; this provides light values against which to contrast the black hull. Again, including the crew members helps indicate the scale of this huge tug.

Puerto Rico, France, Spain, and Iran. Sometimes identical house models were marketed in different states, but often a rendering would be done, photographed, then reworked for a different market, keeping the same floor plan and window sizes. Changing siding materials and colors of roofs, shutters, and brickwork would give a house a new look. There were probably at least 260 Levitt renderings completed in that time span.

The building type almost all American architects designed in the 1980s was the suburban office building. Anyone who has driven through the countryside, particularly in the Northeast, has noticed this new phenomenon of three- to four-story office buildings, surrounded by parking, and sometimes located in office "parks."

Without discussing the sociological significance or the environmental impact, we can touch on their design discipline. Naturally,

Figure 6-11. Williamsburg Bridge renovation. This rendering won an award in the 1988 A.S.A.P. competitive entry traveling show in Los Angeles. Consulting engineers: Ammann & Whitney.

Figure 6-12. Bamm Hollow Country Club in New Jersey. If this seems to have a "September" light, it was unintentional.

Figure 6-13. With the Levitt quad, or a family cluster unit, the marketing objective was to "sell the sizzle" not the steak (in this case hamburger). One didn't need to see endless neighboring units, hence the vignette.

Figure 6-14. Victorian-style house. Rendered for a national house plan publication. Architect: Samuel Paul.

the developers were seeking AAA corporate tenants, and sought to attract them with appropriate architectural sophistication. The design vocabulary of this period was glass—all kinds, granite, precast concrete, and bronze and stainless steel trim. Figure 6–17 shows a fully evolved example of this building type designed by Dan Russell of the Bellemead Development Corp., a subsidiary of the Chubb Corp. The headquarters for Allied Signal (6–19) and the structure in Bohemia New York (6–24) are other examples of that style.

The new Hofstra University Admissions Building's rather complex entrance design called for beginning "inside" with the glass and working outward. As in all tempera work, one needs to have a

Figure 6-15. With the Jefferson School Office Building in Connecticut, the sunlight was taken at an angle that would enhance the appearance of the original decorative brickwork.

good mental image of the finished rendering in order to completely render components with the correct color and values before the over-all rendering takes form.

I have several fascinating German clients. The developer of the building on Maltesestrasse (Figure 6–22), Herr Roland Specker, is an interesting figure on the Berlin scene and through our work I've gotten to know him quite well.

Figure 6-16. Peekskill New York housing development. The uphill-sloping site provided a dark backdrop for the light-colored structure. This sun angle was chosen to emphasize facade detail. Architect: Lloyd Goldfarb.

Figure 6-17. Typical of the hundreds of suburban office buildings built around the country in the 1970s and 1980s is this undulating four-story design by Dan Russell, Architect.

Figure 6-18. Entrance, Computer Sciences Building at University of California, Berkeley. In the bright northern California sunlight the glass was rendered with strong reflections and very little see-through. Architect: Edward Larrabee Barnes, John Ming-Yee Lee, Architects.

In one of our many phone conversations I learned that he too is a runner. When he said he had entered the New York Marathon in 1991, I invited him to join our running club carbo-loading party the night before in a vegetarian restaurant. He really enjoyed meeting some American runners.

He was so enthusiastic about the race that he engaged a taxi on that Saturday to take him along the whole 26-mile race course through the five boroughs—from the start in Staten Island to the fin-

Figure 6-19. This headquarters building for the Allied Signal Company in Pennsylvania has a polished granite facade and a plan configuration presenting plenty of challenge for decisions on reflections, shades, and shadows. Architect, Engineer, and Builder: Schumacher & Forelle.

Figure 6-20. Hofstra University admissions building. Architect: Angelo Francis Corva & Associates.

Figure 6-21.   Buro und Servicezentrum Berlin, Maarienfelde district, 1991. This site is a parallelogram, resulting in a building without 90° corners. German architects design this way on square sites as well. Other design criteria that are different from ours are apparent in this modern office building. Developer: BTG Bautrager Gesellschaft.

ish in Manhattan at Central Park. He had arrived in New York Friday night and was back at his desk in Berlin Monday morning.

I later visited him in Berlin. I'll never lose the image of Roland Specker weaving through fast traffic at night in his light blue Mercedes reading a printout of his favorite restaurants as he called for reservations on the car phone.

Among successful developers, Donald Trump is one of the better known. The Grand Hyatt hotel (Figure 6–25), was his first major project in Manhattan. The old Commodore hotel was an outmoded, soiled, brick building in a neighborhood in decline. Adjacent Grand Central Station, once teeming with long distance travelers, now primarily served commuters, the rest lost to the airlines. The terminal

Figure 6-22.   Maltesestrasse, Berlin, 1991. As in the building opposite, the European design takes some getting used to. This rendering was done using only faxed material in German and, of course, the metric system. Fortunately, the developer, Roland Specker, and his assistant in Berlin spoke excellent English. Developer: Speckergruppe.

itself was filthy, the nearby Chrysler Building in foreclosure, and the money-losing Commodore was destined to close within a year.

All of this didn't make financing easy. Architect Der Scutt was commissioned to create a new hotel out of the gutted Commodore. Renderings were done to sell the new design. The strategies worked: Donald Trump got his tax abatements from the city and financing from the banks.

Trump's creativity proved to be the key to the success of this project. One of these banks was headquartered across the street. *They* wanted the neighborhood to turn around. One newspaper reported that Trump had agreed to finance the cleaning of the Grand Central limestone facade in exchange for sales tax forgiveness on

Figure 6-23. With this Queens New York apartment building by Harmon Jablin, Architects, both sides were lit to better reveal the facade design.

building materials for the construction job. The new-looking terminal could then reflect in the mirror-glass face of the hotel.

The development of Trump Tower was propelled by similar innovative strategies including buying adjacent air rights from Tiffany. Trump Tower is the tallest residential building in New York. It rises straight up 68 stories from the sidewalk in the heart of the most upscale section of Manhattan. *The New York Times* Architecture critic Ada Louise Huxtable called it "a New York block buster of superior design."

Both designs exploited the unique properties of glass—reflections changing constantly as the sun and the clouds move across the sky. Selectivity was important in depicting what images were reflected and how little or how much emphasis they would get. The New York environment affords plenty of opportunity to use whatever reflections make the rendering work.

The Savoy in New York City by Costas Kondylis Architects was

Figure 6-24.   Bohemia New York office building, Long Island. With the glass being painted first, tree locations were planned in preliminary sketches in order to locate their reflections before the trees themselves were rendered. Architect: Mojo Stumer.

later changed from limestone and bronze glass to solar gray and polished stainless steel. The changes were made to the original rendering.

Given the site orientation of the building, the sun could have been taken from the right, or west, side. The floorplan was Y-shaped, and that light direction would have worked as well. The decision to use east sun was made mainly to emphasize the entrance to the building since the retail space on Third Avenue was secondary in importance.

The glass reflections are light at the bottom mirroring the lower lighter sky, then darker going up; they brighten only where the sun's glare comes into play.

Notice the color and value of the white balcony soffits and their reflections in the bronze glass. The sky had to be dark enough to contrast the sunlit concrete structure and light enough to pop the shade side of the tower.

Figure 6-25. The rendering of the Grand Hyatt Hotel in Manhattan was based on a photograph. The bridge was raised so the glass-enclosed restaurant overhanging the sidewalk could be seen. Of course, the soiled Grand Central Station was rendered in steam-cleaned condition. Three-point perspective, though not necessary, was inherited from the photograph and left in.

Figure 6-26. This rendering of Trump Tower is an example of the necessity to remove foreground buildings in a city in order to see the entire project. Architects Swanke Hayden Connell; design architect Der Scutt.

Under most conditions, bronze glass buildings are darker than the sky. They can be deadly dull unless some lighter reflections are introduced. The interesting sawtooth plan of Trump Tower also provided opportunities for lively reflections of reflections.

I was told by a top source that this rendering sold $200 million worth of condominiums—very satisfying.

Figure 6-27. In this Rochester, New York, riverfront building by Davis, Brody & Associates, all glass was rendered in one wash. Then spandrel glass was striped in with a darker transparent wash, using a 3/4″ flat brush. The lighting, the drapery, and the vertical butt joints were done in that order, followed by the half-round polished stainless horizontal mullions. In the site photographs of the Genesee River in the foreground, the riverbed was almost dry and strewn with stumps and boulders. We raised the water level.

Figure 6-28. For 900 Third Avenue by Cesar Pelli and Associates, the Citicorp tower was directly behind the new building. We just moved it to the right. This gave us a bright sunny facade to contrast with the shade side of 900.

Notice how Cesar Pelli used aluminum spandrels to match Hugh Stubbins's low-rise Citicorp element to the left.

The silver reflective glass was rendered with the distorted reflections resulting from "oil canning" I think they're more interesting than flat reflections. They come alive especially as one passes by. Compare the relections shown here with those shown on page 64.

The existing red-painted buildings on the right relate on some level to the red granite on the new building. Again, to allow the ideal view of 900, foreground buildings aren't shown.

Figure 6-29. When an automobile dealer became so successful that he required a Lear jet to visit his out-of-town dealerships, his employees decided to give him a rendering of it for Christmas 1988. It was added to his gallery of automobile showroom renderings.

The 1993 version of Riverside South shows the city-approved scheme by Skidmore Owings & Merrill. The 1993 version of Donald Trump's Riverside South was years in the making (see Figure 6–1), having evolved through stormy debate in the city and local community on New York City's Upper West Side. What planning architects Skidmore Owings & Merrill designed was a scheme of thirteen residential towers on the Hudson River, curving around a park designed by James Balsley Associates. Behind these apartment buildings are commercial office buildings. Railyards formerly occupied the site which stretches from 59th Street to 72nd Street. The West Side Highway will go underground while Riverside Drive will curve inland at the base of the towers.

The view had to encompass the thirteen blocks, and show the park and waterfront to best advantage. The architects had a mass model of the project but not actual building designs. I decided to photograph the model to establish the view. Using a tripod, steel tape, and numerical labels on the model, it was possible to obtain photos with specific height and distance measurements.

Figure 6-30. The Savoy, NY. Projecting balconies are very time-consuming, but the pounce method of transferring them to the board allows the sky wash to flow smoothly, without having to stop at this irregular outline. Clouds help to put the sky behind the building. Costas Kondylis Architects.

Figure 6-31. In this New York Hospital addition by Schuman Lichtenstein Claman and Effron, the shade side of the existing hospital helps to contrast the new building. Again, foreground buildings were eliminated.

Figure 6-32. Office building lobby, 1585 Broadway, New York City.
Interior design: Gensler and Associates; Architect: Gwathmey Siegel.

Figure 6-33. In the new lobby for 40 Wall Street, we have polished granite walls and floor with bold vertical lighting elements reflecting in them. Two horizontal strips of uplighting and uplighting at the tops of the vertical elements were airbrushed. The far end of the space opens to the outside with daylight reflected in the granite wall. The white ceiling receives the glow of the sum total of lighting and reflections. Der Scutt Architect.

Figure 6-34. Retail Arcade, The Bond Building, Sydney, Australia. Kohn Pedersen Fox Architects.

Figure 6-35. Astor Terrace, New York City. Architect: Skidmore Owings & Merrill; Developer: Solomon Equities.

Figure 6-36. Trump Palace by Frank Williams & Associates is a 55-story brick-clad concrete structure on Manhattan's Upper East Side. It's the tallest building north of 59th Street.

The windows reflected the sky, with distant buildings reflecting lighter values than closer ones; the reflections get darker going down the building. Sky reflection gets darker going up until it lightens again as the sky area near the sun is mirrored.

After the distant reflections, balcony slabs and railings were rendered next, then window jambs and heads. Drapery was done with a worn 1/4″ flat brush with a thin wash of yellow ochre and white.

At this scale, I start the drapery about a foot below the window head, where the sun begins to hit it. With larger-scale windows the shaded drapery is rendered in a darker value unless, as in this case, the glass reflections predominate.

As in most renderings of upscale residential buildings, we didn't want just cars on Third Avenue but stretch limos, BMWs, Mercedes, and a Rolls or two—needless to say, there were no garbage trucks or pizza delivery vans.

Figure 6-37. This Sixth Avenue office building in New York City by Swanke Hayden Connell has blue reflective glass and pink granite. The values had to be studied to be sure the building would read against the sky. Background buildings are bland and subdued to make our building pop.

Figure 6-38. The earlier scheme of 343 Sansome Street, San Francisco, by Philip Johnson & John Burgee as viewed from California Street shows a lower existing building just beyond the Bank of California. Real estate considerations were the determining factors in this view. California Street, the Bank of California, and the cable car could mean as much to a potential out-of-town tenant as the Johnson & Burgee design. The view didn't compromise the building itself anyway.

Figure 6-39. This is a rendering of the 270 Madison Avenue rehabilitation by Max Gordon & Associates.

Figure 6-40. 500 Boylston Street, Boston, by Johnson & Burgee.

We settled on a station point 5,100 feet away at an altitude of 1,400 feet on the 77th Street axis. Since the architects had this project in the computer, we sat down and generated a perspective using these numbers. The result was a tidy 43-inch-wide block layout on vellum.

The bad news was that I would have to design the buildings to fit the block model configurations. The idea was to use the Art Deco buildings on Central Park West as a point of departure, so I did photo surveys of them and some research as well. Complicating the process was the fact that as Riverside Drive curves, the buildings do as well, resulting in twelve sets of vanishing points. The layout process was done by color coding five perspective T-squares.

This completed perspective was submitted to the architects who saw the potential in design refinement at this still early phase of the project and proceeded with new studies of each building, faxing them as they progressed. It was worth the extra effort because some original architecture resulted. Even if it all doesn't survive in its

Figure 6-41. Riverside South, New York City, 1993. Skidmore Owings & Merrill, Architects & Planners.

present form, it should stimulate interest in this huge project during a building industry recession in New York.

When the new designs were drawn in perspective they were reviewed by Skidmore Owings & Merrill and refined a bit more. The color work began with some of the background buildings to establish values and tones. Next, the glass on some of the new buildings was put in as a flat blue-black wash. Since they had left the decision about the brick colors up to me, I used Central Park West as a guide, using a range of earth tones and avoiding dark or white brick. In a bird's-eye daytime rendering we don't see interior lighting, so when one is satisfied with the glass value and subtle variations of ground reflections, drapery or blinds can then be rendered.

At this scale, mullions were done with a new brush passing right down the building fast enough to keep the line fine. Mullion shadows on the drapery and jamb reflections were done the same way. The brick returns and sills were rendered in one continuous stroke as well. With the windows complete, the brick spandrels and piers were painted with a brush worn enough to work well for these bands. If the spandrels were recessed, they would be done before the piers, so that the return and its shadow could be done continuously. With each building it was important to maintain contrast with background buildings on dark and sunny sides.

In this rendering there was no attempt to render midtown Manhattan in more than a generic way. At this height of 1,400 feet,

Figure 6-42. Fox & Fowle's rehabilitation of a landmark building in Rochester, New York featured cast iron on one side and masonry on the other.

so much shows that any more would be distracting. I had to select and edit the background elements to portray the character of the West Side in simplified form. The relationship to Central Park was important since it is part of the neighborhood. Riverside Park was painted in the brightest green, since green typically loses intensity in color reproduction. Walks, docks, trees, and people were added. The Hudson River was rendered dark to enhance the brightness of the site. (Take note of the jazz concert in the amphitheater).

The fundamental distinction of night renderings (Figures 6–45, 46) is that the light originates in the building and shines out, instead of the reverse. Obviously, night renderings are desirable when evening use of the building is more significant than daytime use, as in theatres and concert halls—or for dramatic effect for its own sake. Although not shown here, renderers often illustrate the pavement as wet in night renderings to reflect some excitement.

With the renovation of 505 Park Avenue, the night view allowed

Figure 6-43. Lang Suan Ville, a luxury apartment building in Bangkok by Frank Williams & Associates, has design elements well suited for the tempera medium. Buff-colored stucco with white accents reads well against the blue sky. The sky had to have a value darker than the sunny side of the building and a lighter value than the shade side.

Figure 6-44.
St. Charles Cemetery
Mausoleum in Long Island
by Angelo Francis Corva
& Associates is a new
building type — a building
housing 3,000 crypts with
visiting rooms and chapels.
The triangular site was
expressed by indicating
cars on the surrounding
roads.

Figure 6-45. Architect Der Scutt's 505 Park Avenue rehabilitation.

Figure 6-46. Architect Mitchell Newman's glassy Bronx, New York, office building offered a nice challenge in this night view. Clear glass encloses the lobby, while green reflective glass is used on the office facades.

the rendering to emphasize the uplighting at the base of the facade treatment. The polished brass could reflect both the uplighting and neighboring buildings. The retail area at the base of the building could also be shown in detail. The idea of the night rendering was chosen to better highlight the retail space and to depict the exterior lighting.

For 555 Fifth Avenue, the rendering illustrates a 1994 facade treatment for a 1950s office building. The original white brick building with single-glazed steel windows was no longer competitive in the midtown New York rental market of the 90s. This new skin was designed to present the building as energy efficient, up-to-date; and note the greenhouse-type fenestration added to the setbacks.

The architect asked that street activity in the rendering be kept to a minimum in order to focus attention on the office space above. Because the current retail tenant was staying on, there was no need to emphasize the street activity to sell the retail space. The adjacent

Figure 6-47. This rendering is of Gwathmey Siegel's Port Washington Library addition. The off-white concrete structure called for a dark blue sky for contrast especially since in black and white reproductions the blue would reproduce lighter than its actual value. This rendering was done for fund-raising purposes along with interior depictions of the new concert hall and art gallery.

551 Fifth Avenue structure was rendered, then airbrushed to subordinate it to 555 Fifth Avenue.

As perhaps an indication of how hard and long renderers work, the 117 illustrations in this book represent about six percent of the number of Baehr renderings done in the corresponding years.

The good news is that each new assignment offers a fresh challange to make a good statement about architecture.

Figure 6-48. 555 Fifth Avenue. Der Scutt Architect.

7

Gallery of Contemporary Tempera Work

■ This chapter presents some representative examples of the current or recent work of some other tempera renderers.

Robert Cook is president of Prelim, Inc., a rendering studio in Dallas in operation for over thirty years. They specialize in tempera, serving clients nationwide and abroad. These renderings were each produced by two or three artists using their unique talents to achieve the special effects.

Figure 7-1. City Trust multi-use project.
Architect: Design Collaborative, Bridgeport, CT.

Figure 7-2. San Antonio office tower addition.
Architect: Steve McWilliams.

Figure 7-3. International Plaza Lobby, Seattle, WA.
Architect: Curtis Beattie, AIA, Seattle.
Designer: Warner Boone, Honolulu.

Emil Kempa, an architect and renderer, is a graduate of The Columbia University School of Architecture. He practiced architecture as a principal in the architectural firm of Kempa and Schwartz. He did his rendering originally in the office of Furno, Kempa, and Schwartz and later on his own in New York City.

Figure 7-4. Indiana University Law School addition.
Architect: The Eggers Group, New York; Odle/Burke, Bloomington, Indiana.

Figure 7-5. Entrance to the Palace Hotel, New York City. Architect: Emery Roth & Sons.

Figure 7-6. World Trade Center office building, New York City.
Architect: Emery Roth & Sons.

Russ Moore, after graduating from the Cranbrook Academy of Art, worked in the studios of various illustrators before he joined George Cooper Rudolph's architectural rendering office in New York City. Since then, he has practiced on his own in Garden City and Forest Hills, New York.

Figure 7-7. Proposed office building, Columbus Circle, New York City. Original conception by Russ Moore.

Figure 7-8. Proposed office building, 42nd Street and Fifth Avenue, New York City. Original conception by Russ Moore.

Thomas Pepper graduated from Syracuse University, BFA, then gravitated to architectural rendering. He worked for a time in the office of Furno, Kempa, and Schwartz in New York. Since that time, he has had an individual practice on Long Island using pen and ink, pencil, and watercolor, but primarily tempera.

Figure 7-9. Converted landmark building, Long Island, New York. Architect: Warren Schiffman.

Figure 7-10. Vietnam War Memorial, competition winner, Farmingville, New York. Architectural Designer: Robert D. Fox.

Robert E. Schwartz AIA graduated from the Columbia University School of Architecture and went into practice as an architect and renderer in the office of Furno, Kempa, and Schwartz. He and Emil Kempa did much of the rendering work for many of the large New York firms from 1953 to 1973. Since that time, Mr. Schwartz has practiced architecture in Greenwich, CT.

Figure 7-11. Hotel, tennis club, and convention center Warwick Parrish, Bermuda. Architect: Robert E. Schwartz.

Index

Index of Renderings